# BREAKING THE CYCLE OF IRRATIONAL FEAR

FROM "WHAT IF" TO "WHAT IS"

KEDEISHA S. FOUNTAIN

Edited by
NICOLE QUEEN

VISION PUBLISHING
H O U S E

Vision Publishing House
support@vision-publishinghouse.com
www.vision-publishinghouse.com

ISBN: 978-1-955297-68-4 (print)

This book is established to provide information and inspiration to all readers. It is designed with the understanding that the author is not engaged to render any psychological, legal, or any other kind of professional advice. The content is the sole expression of the author. The author is not liable for any physical, psychological, emotional, financial, or commercial damages, including, but not limited to special, incidental, consequential, or other damages. All readers are responsible for their own choices, actions, and results.

# CONTENTS

# INTRODUCTION

This brief guide is designed for those struggling with fear, often masked as anxiety, worry, concern, unease, apprehension, nervousness, and dread. This guide encourages readers to avoid hypotheticals and focus on the reality of the situation. When faced with triggering events, it is common for those entertaining fear to fixate on unknown possibilities. However, a focus on factual information can significantly ease anxiety.

Dedicated to my fellow therapists, this book provides succinct, effective techniques to help clients conquer a fear-driven mentality. It also serves as an essential resource for anyone struggling with fear, offering practical strategies for managing emotions swiftly and effectively.

Central to this guide is the acronym F.E.A.R., which serves as the foundational framework for this guide. Each chapter is dedicated to a specific component of this framework, delving deeply into interconnected themes that define our experiences of fear.

- The first chapter focuses on *Feelings*, exploring the nuanced sensations that accompany fear and how they are exhibited in our bodies.

- The second chapter, *Emotions*, examines how physiological responses, behavioral reactions, and cognitive appraisals collectively shape our emotional states in fear.

- The third chapter, *Anxiety*, explores fear in the context of future uncertainties, focusing on the 'what if' scenarios that often provoke anxiety.

- The fourth chapter, *Reality*, helps readers differentiate between perceived threats and real-world facts, providing practical strategies to effectively manage and mitigate fear.

By guiding you through these fundamental aspects of F.E.A.R. — *Feelings, Emotions, Anxiety,* and *Reality* — this book aims to equip you with the tools needed to understand and effectively manage fear, transforming it from a hindrance into a catalyst for personal growth.

# 1

## FEELINGS

F ear is a primal emotion that serves as a crucial survival mechanism, alerting us to potential threats and dangers. In this guide, we explore the 'F' in fear, which we will define as 'feelings' for the purpose of our discussion. Understanding our feelings associated with fear is essential as they can profoundly influence our behaviors and decisions. Fear is not just an emotion; it activates a host of physical responses that prepare our bodies to react to danger.

### Recognize and Label Physical Responses

Let's delve into how fear, as an emotion, triggers physical responses such as an increased heart rate or the urge to flee from the situation causing the fear. It is the conscious experience of being afraid. Interestingly, even though your feelings cause a physical response, this does not necessarily mean that what you are experiencing is true (LeDoux, J. E., 1996, *The Emotional Brain: The Mysterious Underpinnings of Emotional Life*).

**Explore 'What If' Scenarios**

Our minds often create scenarios that fuel our anxieties, especially when we find ourselves in distressing situations. For example, imagine your dog Rocky ran away from home, and you eventually found him. During the search, you might experience a surge of physical reactions, such as an increased heart rate and intense anxiety. These reactions are often linked to troubling thoughts like, "What if someone found Rocky before I did?" This illustrates how our physical responses can be directly tied to 'what if' thoughts—mental distortions that lack solid evidence but trigger real physical responses. Understanding this dynamic is crucial in learning to manage our fears more effectively by recognizing them as reactions to hypothetical, not actual, scenarios.

**Increase Awareness of Unique Feelings**

It's essential for therapists to help their clients develop a deeper awareness of the connections between their thoughts and physical sensations. Encourage your clients to recognize that their physical reactions often stem from 'what if' thoughts, which manifest as tangible responses in their bodies.

By exploring these 'what if' scenarios and noting their associated physical reactions, clients can gain valuable insights into how these thoughts impact them physically. This increased awareness of their bodily responses not only deepens their understanding of their emotional and psychological triggers but also empowers them to be more effective in making positive changes. Understanding these dynamics is crucial for clients to manage their reactions and ultimately transform their fear into a more constructive and manageable emotion.

While some theories, such as those proposed by Paul Ekman (Ekman, P., 1999. *Basic Emotions*), argue that certain basic emotions are universal, the subjective experience of these emotions can vary significantly among individuals. Carl Rogers, in his seminal work, *On Becoming a Person: A Therapist's View of Psychotherapy* (Rogers, 1961), emphasized the unique, personal nature of each individual's emotional experience. He asserted that each person's feelings are shaped by their perceptions and life experiences. This perspective is crucial for therapists to acknowledge and validate each client's distinct emotional responses, further enhancing the therapeutic process by recognizing the individuality of emotional experiences.

---

*Turn the page to access the supplemental worksheets for this chapter to enhance your understanding and application of the concepts discussed.*

**Worksheet: Recognize and Label Physical Responses**

*Objective*: To increase awareness of physical responses to fear

1. Describe a recent situation where you felt fear. What physical responses did you experience (e.g., increased heart rate, sweating)?

_____

_____

_____

_____

_____

_____

_____

_____

_____

_____

_____

2. Label these responses. Write down each physical response and label it (e.g., "sweating = fear").

_____

_____

_____

_____

_____

_____

_____

_____

_____

_____

**Worksheet: Explore "What If" Scenarios**

*Objective*: To understand how "what if" scenarios impact physical reactions

1. Identify a 'what if' thought you had recently.

_____
_____
_____
_____
_____
_____
_____
_____
_____
_____

2. How did this thought make you feel physically? Compare these physical reactions to those from an actual event.

_____
_____
_____
_____
_____
_____
_____
_____
_____
_____
_____

**Worksheet: Increase Awareness of Unique Feelings**

*Objective*: To recognize the connection between "what if" thoughts and physical responses

1. Keep a daily log of your "what if" thoughts and the corresponding physical reactions.

_____

_____

_____

_____

_____

_____

_____

_____

_____

_____

2. What patterns do you notice? How do these thoughts and reactions affect your daily life?

_____

_____

_____

_____

_____

_____

_____

_____

_____

_____

# 2

## EMOTIONS

I n our exploration of fear, the "E" represents emotions, which are intricate psychological states comprising physiological responses, behavioral responses, and cognitive appraisals, as discussed by Lazarus in *Emotion and Adaptation* (1991). Having previously addressed the physiological aspects of emotions when discussing feelings, we will now focus on understanding behavioral responses and cognitive appraisals.

### Identify Behavioral Responses

Behavioral responses are the actions we take in response to our emotions, which can range from avoidance to confrontation, depending on the individual and the situation. This segment aims to dissect these reactions and the mental evaluations that accompany them, providing insights into how our perceptions and feelings influence our behaviors.

**Recondition Thought Patterns**

Understanding and modifying our thought patterns is crucial for managing how we respond to fear and anxiety. Clients must first identify the behavioral responses that stem from 'what if' thoughts. These types of thoughts often trigger emotional responses, which then manifest as specific behaviors. According to the principle "I think, therefore I act," our actions are greatly influenced by our thoughts, including those that are not based on facts.

This concept, elaborated by Beck in *Cognitive Therapy and Emotional Disorders* (1979), illustrates how negative thought patterns can condition the brain to respond in certain ways. By reconditioning these thought patterns, clients can learn to interrupt and reshape their habitual responses to fear, leading to more adaptive behaviors and improved emotional regulation.

**Understand Cognitive Appraisal**

Cognitive appraisal is a fundamental concept in understanding how individuals interpret and respond to different situations emotionally and behaviorally. Reflecting on my college years, I recall learning about classical conditioning, a process first described by Ivan Pavlov. This learning mechanism involves associations formed between an environmental stimulus and a naturally occurring stimulus, as discussed in Pavlov's seminal work, *Conditioned Reflexes: An Investigation of the Physiological Activity of the Cerebral Cortex* (1927).

As therapists, our aim is to assist clients in reconditioning their thought processes. By encouraging them to think differently, we can help align their behavioral responses with reality instead of hypothetical 'what if' scenarios. This cognitive shift is crucial for breaking the cycle of negative thought patterns and fostering healthier, more accurate responses to the challenges they face.

*Cognitive Appraisal: A Key to Managing Fear and Anxiety*

Cognitive appraisal is the mental process through which we interpret and label our emotions, such as identifying feelings of fear or joy. In this book, we specifically address the kind of fear that often manifests as anxiety, which can significantly hinder an individual's ability to manage daily activities. This psychological process can be segmented into two distinct phases: primary appraisal, where an individual assesses whether an event is a threat, and secondary appraisal, where the individual evaluates their own capacity to cope with the threat.

Understanding and effectively navigating these appraisal stages are crucial for clients striving to mitigate anxiety and enhance their overall emotional resilience. This focus aims to provide strategies that help clients recognize their emotional triggers and thoughtfully respond to them, thus managing fear more effectively.

*Primary Appraisal*

Primary appraisal is the initial step in the cognitive appraisal process, where clients learn to evaluate and categorize their experiences. This stage involves assisting clients in assessing a situation to determine its relevance to their well-being. They are taught to discern whether an event is irrelevant, meaning it has no significant emotional impact; benign-positive, indicating that it may have a favorable outcome; or stressful, suggesting a potential threat or challenge.

*Secondary Appraisal*

Secondary appraisal is a critical phase in the cognitive appraisal process where clients assess their ability to cope with identified stressors. This stage involves guiding clients to evaluate the resources they have available to manage the stressor, such as personal strengths, social support systems, and practical tools. Clients are also encouraged to consider the potential outcomes of different coping strategies.

Understanding cognitive appraisal is fundamental for therapists aiming to assist their clients in identifying and modifying maladaptive thought patterns. By focusing on how clients appraise their 'what if' scenarios— those hypothetical situations that often trigger anxiety — therapists can guide them toward developing more adaptive emotional and behavioral responses.

This shift in appraisal is a central tenet of Cognitive Behavioral Therapy (CBT), which emphasizes the transformation of negative thought patterns as a pathway to enhanced emotional well-being and improved behavioral outcomes. Through CBT, clients learn to challenge and reframe their perceptions of potential threats, reducing anxiety and fostering a more balanced and positive outlook. This process not only helps in managing immediate stressors but also builds long-term resilience by equipping clients with skills to handle future challenges more effectively.

*Turn the page to access the supplemental worksheets for this chapter to enhance your understanding and application of the concepts discussed.*

**Worksheet: Identify Behavioral Responses**

*Objective*: To recognize how emotions trigger behaviors

1. Describe a recent situation where you felt a strong emotion.

_____

_____

_____

_____

_____

_____

_____

_____

_____

_____

_____

2. What behaviors followed this emotion?

_____

_____

_____

_____

_____

_____

_____

_____

_____

_____

_____

_____

**Worksheet: Recondition Thought Patterns**

*Objective*: To change negative thought patterns

1. Identify a negative thought you often have. What behavior does this thought trigger?

_____

_____

_____

_____

_____

_____

_____

_____

_____

2. Write a more positive or realistic version of this thought.

_____

_____

_____

_____

_____

_____

_____

_____

_____

_____

_____

**Worksheet: Understand Cognitive Appraisal**

*Objective*: To learn to appraise situations more accurately

1. Think of a stressful situation you faced recently. How did you appraise it initially (primary appraisal)?

_____

_____

_____

_____

_____

_____

2. What resources did you identify to handle it (secondary appraisal)?

_____

_____

_____

_____

_____

_____

3. How can you apply this appraisal process to future situations?

_____

_____

_____

_____

_____

_____

# ANXIETY

In the treatment of anxiety, a significant challenge is the tendency to focus on future uncertainties or potential negative outcomes, commonly known as 'what if' scenarios. David H. Barlow in his seminal work, *Anxiety and Its Disorders: The Nature and Treatment of Anxiety and Panic* (2002), emphasizes how anxiety often arises from fears about what might happen rather than what is currently happening. To counteract this, clients and therapists must collaboratively work to anchor thoughts in the present moment.

## Stay Focused on the Present

The present is the only time where facts can be identified and validated. By concentrating on what is directly observable and factual, clients can reduce the impact of unfounded fears about future events or outcomes, which often have no basis in the reality of 'now.' This practice not only helps in managing anxiety but also enhances overall mental clarity and emotional stability.

**Eliminate Irrational Fear**

Managing irrational fear effectively requires understanding its roots and manifestations. Anxiety, while experienced in the present, often stems from worries about the future. These fears are typically driven by 'what if' thoughts, which create anxiety by focusing on potential negative outcomes rather than what is currently happening. Therapists play a crucial role in helping clients break this cycle by guiding them to remain anchored in the present moment, avoiding projections into the future. This approach encourages clients to focus on verifiable facts rather than hypothetical scenarios.

As noted by Williams, Teasdale, Segal, and Kabat-Zinn in *The Mindful Way through Depression: Freeing Yourself from Chronic Unhappiness* (2007), concentrating on facts helps clients stay grounded in reality, steering them toward their desired outcomes without being swayed by a distorted perception of reality. This method is integral to overcoming anxiety and fostering a stable, fact-based approach to daily challenges.

**Gather and Rely on Facts**

In cognitive therapy, a fundamental approach to managing anxiety involves the careful collection and consideration of factual information. Therapists aim to guide their clients away from irrational fears by focusing on gathering facts that affirm the reality of their current situation. This practice is crucial for disarming the often paralyzing 'what if' scenarios that fuel anxiety. By concentrating on what is factual and present, clients can significantly reduce speculative anxieties, thus remaining anchored in the present moment.

This method not only represents a strategic approach to handling anxiety but also promotes a healthier, more grounded mindset, as articulated by Wells in *Cognitive Therapy of Anxiety Disorders: A Practice Manual and Conceptual Guide* (1997). Engaging with the actualities of their experiences helps clients cultivate a more stable emotional state and fosters resilience against future uncertainties.

---

*Turn the page to access the supplemental worksheets for this chapter to enhance your understanding and application of the concepts discussed.*

**Worksheet: Stay Focused on the Present**

*Objective*: To practice staying in the moment to reduce anxiety

1. Describe a recent situation where you felt anxious about the future. What were your "what if" thoughts?

_____

_____

_____

_____

_____

_____

_____

_____

_____

_____

_____

_____

2. What facts could you focus on to stay in the present?

_____

_____

_____

_____

_____

_____

_____

_____

_____

_____

_____

_____

**Worksheet: Eliminate Irrational Fear**

*Objective*: To recognize and eliminate irrational fears

1. Identify an irrational fear you have.

_____

_____

_____

_____

_____

_____

_____

_____

_____

_____

_____

2. What evidence do you have that supports this fear? What evidence contradicts it?

_____

_____

_____

_____

_____

_____

_____

_____

_____

_____

_____

_____

**Worksheet: Gather and Rely on Facts**

*Objective*: To use facts to ground yourself in reality

1. Choose a recent fear or worry. List all the facts related to this fear.

_____

_____

_____

_____

_____

_____

_____

_____

_____

_____

_____

2. How do these facts change your perception of the fear?

_____

_____

_____

_____

_____

_____

_____

_____

_____

_____

_____

_____

_____

# 4

# REALITY

The concept of 'what if' scenarios can significantly distort our perception of reality. These hypothetical thoughts alter the brain's information-processing mechanisms, instigating fear and anxiety in the absence of any real threat. This type of anxiety is rooted in false premises, essentially rewiring the brain to trust an emotional response driven by distorted thinking. Specifically, the right amygdala— an area of the brain closely linked to negative emotions—becomes particularly active during these episodes.

However, there is hope. The brain can be rewired to diminish or altogether eliminate 'what if' thinking that often projects fears onto future or potential events. Cognitive Behavioral Therapy (CBT) has proven to be a highly effective treatment method in tackling anxiety that stems from these fear-based thoughts.

To support this cognitive restructuring, several strategies can be implemented to retrain the brain, including:

- Exercising
- Meditating
- Practicing gratitude

- Reframing negative thoughts

These activities foster a more positive and present-focused mindset that enhances emotional well-being and reality-based perceptions. Let's examine the benefits of each.

## Exercise

- *Physical Benefits*: Engaging in regular physical activity not only enhances overall health, but also significantly reduces the risk of chronic diseases, which contributes to a stronger and more resilient body.

- *Mental Health Benefits*: Exercise is also a powerful tool for mental health, as it stimulates the release of endorphins—natural mood lifters that elevate well-being. Additionally, it lowers the levels of stress hormones such as adrenaline and cortisol, providing a calming effect on the mind.

- *Cognitive Effects*: Beyond physical and mental health, exercise plays a crucial role in cognitive function. It can sharpen memory and improve overall cognitive abilities, effectively breaking the cycle of negative thought patterns, as discussed by Ratey and Hagerman in their influential work, *Spark: The Revolutionary New Science of Exercise and the Brain* (2008).

## Meditation

- *Mindfulness*: Meditation practices are key in helping individuals stay present and focused. By encouraging a moment-to-moment awareness, meditation reduces the tendency to worry about the future, enabling a more engaged and attentive experience of the present

- *Stress Reduction*: Regular meditation significantly decreases stress and anxiety levels. It promotes relaxation and emotional stability, which are crucial for overall well-being and effective stress management.

- *Neuroplasticity*: Meditation also contributes to structural changes in the brain, specifically through the increase of grey matter density. This growth occurs in areas associated with emotional regulation and self-control, highlighting the profound impact of meditation on mental health. This neuroplastic effect is well-documented in the study by B. K. Hölzel et al. (2011), *Mindfulness Practice Leads to Increases in Regional Brain Gray Matter Density*, published in Psychiatry Research: Neuroimaging.

## Gratitude

- *Positive Focus*: Practicing gratitude helps shift the focus from negative to positive aspects of life, cultivating a more optimistic outlook. This change in perspective encourages individuals to appreciate the good in their daily experiences, enhancing overall contentment.

- *Emotional Well-being*: Engaging in practicing gratitude has profound long-term effects on emotional health. Studies have shown that regular gratitude exercises are associated with higher levels of happiness and reduced instances of depression and anxiety, contributing to greater emotional resilience.

- *Social Benefits:* Expressing gratitude strengthens relationships and fosters a sense of community by enhancing social bonds and support, which are vital for maintaining mental health. This aspect is supported by research from Emmons and McCullough, who in their 2003 study, *Counting Blessings versus Burdens: An Experimental Investigation of Gratitude and Subjective Well-being in Daily Life*, demonstrated how gratitude can lead to increased subjective well-being in daily life, underscoring its importance in social interactions.

## Reframing Negative Thoughts

- *Cognitive Restructuring:* This technique focuses on identifying and challenging negative thought patterns. By systematically replacing these unhelpful thoughts with more balanced and rational alternatives, clients can begin to see and interpret their situations more clearly and positively.

- *Emotional Regulation:* Alongside cognitive restructuring, reframing plays a critical role in emotional regulation. It helps clients better manage their emotions by decreasing the intensity of negative feelings. This process not only makes challenging situations more manageable, but also enhances overall emotional resilience.

- *Behavioral Changes:* The alteration of thought patterns through cognitive restructuring and emotional regulation naturally leads to behavioral changes. By modifying how they think and feel, clients are able to enact positive changes in their behavior, which subsequently improve their daily interactions and outcomes. These concepts are explored in Beck's *Cognitive Behavior Therapy: Basics and Beyond* (2011), which provides a foundational guide for these therapeutic techniques.

The key lies in recognizing that irrational thoughts are not based in reality. For meaningful change to occur, clients must first acknowledge that their fears are unreasonable. Therapists and clients can then collaborate effectively, using various tools to dismantle irrational 'what if' thoughts and reconstruct more rational thought patterns.

*Turn the page to access the supplemental worksheets for this chapter to enhance your understanding and application of the concepts discussed.*

**Worksheet: Reality**

*Objective*: To use physical activity to improve mental health

1. Describe your current exercise routine. How does exercise make you feel physically and mentally?

_____

_____

_____

_____

_____

_____

_____

_____

_____

_____

_____

2. Set a goal to increase your physical activity this week.

_____

_____

_____

_____

_____

_____

_____

_____

_____

_____

_____

**Worksheet: Meditation**

*Objective*: To incorporate mindfulness practices into your daily routine

1. Try a short meditation session. How did you feel before and after the session?

_____

_____

_____

_____

_____

_____

_____

_____

_____

_____

2. Set a goal to meditate daily for a week.

_____

_____

_____

_____

_____

_____

_____

_____

_____

_____

_____

**Worksheet: Gratitude**

*Objective*: To foster a positive mindset through gratitude

1. List three things you are grateful for today.

_____

_____

_____

_____

_____

_____

_____

_____

_____

_____

_____

_____

2. How does focusing on gratitude change your mood? Make a daily habit of writing down things you are grateful for.

_____

_____

_____

_____

_____

_____

_____

_____

_____

_____

_____

_____

**Worksheet: Reframing Negative Thoughts**

*Objective*: To replace negative thoughts with positive ones

1. Identify a negative thought you had today. Reframe it into a positive or more realistic thought.

_____

_____

_____

_____

_____

_____

_____

_____

_____

_____

_____

2. How does this new thought make you feel?

_____

_____

_____

_____

_____

_____

_____

_____

_____

_____

_____

_____

## 5

# FINAL THOUGHTS

By understanding and applying the principles outlined in this guide, therapists can effectively assist their clients in moving beyond anxiety driven by 'what if' scenarios. Focusing on the present and employing therapeutic techniques helps foster a healthier mind-set, significantly enhancing clients' emotional well-being and overall quality of life.

Encouraging practices such as exercise, meditation, gratitude, and reframing negative thoughts can lead to lasting changes. As therapists, our role is crucial in guiding clients through this transformative process, aiding them in recognizing the irrational nature of their fears and establishing a foundation of rational, reality-based thinking.

This focus on the present and debunking the distortions of 'what if' thinking empowers clients to achieve a more balanced and peaceful state of mind, ultimately breaking the cycle of irrational fear and anxiety.

*Turn the page to access the supplemental worksheets for this chapter to enhance your understanding and application of the concepts discussed.*

**Worksheet: Final Thoughts**

*Objective*: To summarize what you have learned and set goals for the future

1. Reflect on the strategies you have learned in this book. Which strategies were most effective for you? How will you incorporate these strategies into your daily life?

_____

_____

_____

_____

_____

_____

_____

_____

_____

2. Set three specific goals to help manage your anxiety and fear. What steps will you take to achieve these goals? How will you measure your progress?

_____

_____

_____

_____

_____

_____

_____

_____

_____

# REFERENCES

Barlow, D. H. (2002). *Anxiety and Its Disorders: The Nature and Treatment of Anxiety and Panic.*

Beck, A. T. (1979). *Cognitive Therapy and the Emotional Disorders.*

Beck, J. S. (2011). *Cognitive Behavior Therapy: Basics and Beyond.*

Emmons, R. A., & McCullough, M. E. (2003). Counting blessings versus burdens: An experimental investigation of gratitude and subjective well-being in daily life. *Journal of Personality and Social Psychology.*

Ekman, P. (1999). *Basic Emotions.*

Hölzel, B. K., et al. (2011). Mindfulness practice leads to increases in regional brain gray matter density. *Psychiatry Research: Neuroimaging.*

Lazarus, R. S. (1991). *Emotion and Adaptation.*

LeDoux, J. E. (1996). *The Emotional Brain: The Mysterious Underpinnings of Emotional Life.*

Rogers, C. (1961). *On Becoming a Person: A Therapist's View of Psychotherapy.*

Pavlov, I. P. (1927). *Conditioned Reflexes: An Investigation of the Physiological Activity of the Cerebral Cortex.*

Ratey, J. J., & Hagerman, E. (2008). *Spark: The Revolutionary New Science of Exercise and the Brain.*

Wells, A. (1997). *Cognitive Therapy of Anxiety Disorders: A Practice Manual and Conceptual Guide.*

Williams, M., Teasdale, J., Segal, Z., & Kabat-Zinn, J. (2007). *The Mindful Way through Depression: Freeing Yourself from Chronic Unhappiness.*

# ABOUT THE AUTHOR

Kedeisha S. Fountain is a licensed professional counselor committed to enhancing emotional and spiritual well-being through a holistic approach. By integrating her clients' beliefs into therapy, she creates personalized experiences that respect their unique perspectives.

Kedeisha's professional background spans counseling roles in skilled nursing facilities, senior homes, and extensive case management. Certified as a brain injury specialist, she has worked diligently to positively impact the lives of those she has had the privilege to assist.

Utilizing strength-based and client-centered methods, Kedeisha fosters a supportive, collaborative environment. She specializes in treating a variety of challenges, including anxiety, depression, trauma, and relationship issues, and provides both faith-based and general counseling services.

Kedeisha's compassionate support empowers clients to embrace their strengths and embark on a transformative journey toward holistic well-being.

To get in touch with Kedeisha S. Fountain, please contact her here:

Email: mindaftermind21@gmail.com
Website: www.mindaftermind.com

www.ingramcontent.com/pod-product-compliance
Lightning Source LLC
Chambersburg PA
CBHW051600120626
46551CB00013B/1600